Markov Models

Master the Unsupervised

Machine Learning in Python

and Data Science with

Hidden Markov Models and

Real World Applications

By: Robert Wilson

Table of Contents

RANDOM TEXT GENERATOR

SINGLE SPEAKER WORD RECOGNITION

CONCLUSION

Introduction

If reading about Markov models, stochastic processes, and probabilities leaves you scratching your head, then you have definitely come to the right place.

If you are looking for the most no-nonsense guide that will keep you on the right course during the turbulent ride filled with scientific enigmas, machine learning, and predicting probabilities of hidden, unobservable states, then you have found your perfect companion.

Stepping away from the usual explanations and diving a little bit deeper into the essence of not only the definition and implementation of the Markov models but also the process of building and training them for best results, this book will help anyone master data science effortlessly.

This is not a geek-only book. This guide is written anyone who knows a thing or two about Python programming and had a passing Math grade in high school.

Learning the power of probabilities, building models, and training them to perfection to master some of the most popular Markov models' real-life applications, this is the best scientific eye-opener you will ever find.

Learning Without Supervision

If the term 'machine learning' plants an image of a robot inside your head, you are not far away from the truth. Machine learning means exactly what the name itself suggests, machines that are able to learn. What does that mean? That means that machines can learn on their own even when they are not programmed for that purpose.

Machine learning, the computer science field that has altered the world of technology completely, is the ability of the computer programs to change when being exposed to new, unfamiliar data. With the help of algorithms that learn from data iteratively, this type of artificial intelligence makes it possible for computers to find a solution for their problems despite the fact that they are not programmed to do so. How does it work?

By receiving new data computers are left to make predictions on their own in order to find the right answer. Machine learning is the field that is used in those situations when it is impossible to simply write a program and create a particular algorithm.

Learning from new and unfamiliar data means learning from examples. This is a lot easier in non-machine learning when there are precise algorithms, each with a different job, and all working towards finding the right answer. In machine learning, there is no such thing as precise algorithms.

So how do they learn? Although there are more than two types of machine learning methods, there are two main ways in which machines can learn: with supervision and without supervision.

Supervised machine learning is often referred to as learning with a teacher. In this case, there is a 'teacher' that provides label data to the machine. The machine uses the labeled data to later discover things on its own, and learn from examples. Here, the machines know how and what to look for.

Unsupervised machine learning, as you might have already guessed is a little bit harder to accomplish, since here, there is no teacher and the machines are left to do all of the work by themselves. That means there is no labeled data or other indicators that may hint the computer which direction is the right way to go. Instead, the computer tries to take advantage of those patterns that frequently reoccur in data. Since there are no hints and labeled data to work with, machines try to find the right answer by figuring out what commonly occurs in data, and then comparing it with what occurs uncommonly.

Unlike supervised learning that provides targets for all new inputs, in unsupervised learning there is a limited set of inputs that machines have to work with. To try and find the right answer on their own, without supervision, machines use many different methods. The most common and probably the most important one of all, is clustering, which is basically grouping things together in order to solve the problem.

To explain this, I will use a simple, non-technical example. Let's imagine that you have a basket filled with different fruits and your job is to arrange the fruits from the same type at one place. In supervised learning, there is a teacher that trains you to learn the shape and color of the fruit types by feeding you the information earlier, so you can solve the problem when necessary. By having the knowledge that if a particular fruit has so and so features is let's say apple, it is easy for you to classify the fruits from the basket.

But what happens if you have never seen a fruit before? What if you know absolutely nothing about the fruits from the basket and there is no labeled data to work with? In unsupervised learning, you have to figure out the answer on your own. For instance, you may first decide to group them based on their color. So, you take the red fruits like apples and strawberries and group them together. You take the green ones like grapes and pears and make another group. Then, you take another physical category into consideration, such as size. So, green color – pears, red fruits – strawberries, and so on. Then you may consider their shape. Rounded shape with a depression – apples, cone shape with a green 'hat' – strawberries. Finally, you combine all three of these characteristics and determine the fruits that belong to the same fruit type.

Sure, apples can be both green and red, and not all strawberries are cone-shaped, but I believe this was a good example that can help you grasp what unsupervised learning really is. Unsupervised machine learning makes prediction with the help of their built-in models with the same inputs. Today, we are going to focus on the Markov models and how you can use them for solving problems when you don't have enough clues to work with.

Explaining Markov Models

By definition, Markov models are stochastic models used for modeling randomly changed systems where the next state depends on the previous and the previous state alone. Markov models are not interested in what was in the past, they are just concerned with the one before the state they want to predict. To understand this better, think of them as models with no memory. For instance, imagine that you have just arrived in a town and it is sunny. You have no knowledge of what the weather was like the day before or the day before that. You only know the current state which is sunny weather so you predict what the weather will be like tomorrow based only on that fact.

Markov models are similar to this. They are based on the Markov processes which only analyze dependent states that depend solely on the state that happened last. This is also often referred to as Markov assumption and it is really a strong one. You have to throw out everything that happened in the past, all the historic data, and take only the current state into consideration in order to predict what will happen next.

Many confuse tossing a coin with this. If you get 'Heads' now, what is the probability of getting 'Tails' next? It may sound similar, but tossing a coin that gathers 'Heads' and 'Tails' sequences has nothing to do with Markov models. Why? Because 'Heads' and 'Tails' are not dependent states. The fact that you have just tossed 'Heads' has nothing to do with the 'Tails' that you tossed earlier. What the weather will be like tomorrow, on the other hand, is dependent on today's weather, and that is a perfect Markov model example.

How Do They Predict?

Markov models don't use crystal balls in order to predict future states, but probabilities. If math wasn't your strong suit in high school and you already feel intimidated, don't be. The mathematics behind these Markov models are not as complex as they may seem, and this chapter will convince you in that.

Let's say that you have a baby and you are planning a picnic for this afternoon. The weather forecast says that it will be sunny all day long, so there is nothing that can ruin the perfect day. Oh, except a baby's mood is changed more than their diapers. So, how to know if your baby will be a sleepy angel or a crying machine? Should you bring a bag full of toys to keep her occupied, or will the fresh air keep her calm and happy?

To crack this puzzle, we will need to know all of the 'states' that the baby can go into. Supposing that the baby is not hungry and her diaper is dry, the baby can be either calm, upset, or asleep.

In order for us to predict what the baby's mood will be this afternoon based on how the baby is feeling now, we need to have a good grasp of the math behind the Markov model's probabilities (again, not as complex as it sounds).

Like we said, the Markov assumption, also referred to as Markov property, is that the future state depends solely on the current state, and the current state is a result of the previous state alone. That means that the distribution of the states at time t depends solely on the state at time *t-1*.

To put it mathematically:

$$P\left(s_t / s_{t-1}\right)$$

If we were about to make a more general assumption and consider that the current state was a result of a sequence of previous states, meaning that the distribution of the current state depends on all of the past states, the formula would be:

$$P\left(s_t / s_{t-1}, s_{t-2}, s_{t-3}, \ldots, s_0\right)$$

But, since neither s_t-2 nor s_{t-3} give us useful information about s_t, this comes down to:

$$P\left(s_t / s_{t-1}, s_{t-2}, s_{t-3}, \ldots, s_0\right) = P\left(s_t / s_{t-1}\right)$$

And in case you are wondering, no, I did not use the previous states as a mean to confuse you, but to help you see the whole specific sequence in order for you to be able to understand how and why the joint probability is modeled.

$$P(s_t, s_{t-1}, ..., s_1, s_0) = P(s_t / s_{t-1}, ..., s_0) \ P(s_{t-1} / s_{t-2}, ..., s_0) ... P(s_0)$$

This is a consequence of the Bayes rule (Remember from high school? Bayes rule helps us determine the conditional probability in those cases when we don't know what the joint probability is)

$$P(s_1, s_0) = P(s_1 / s_0) P(s_0)$$

Now, assuming that the Markov property in this case is true, we can simplify it to:

$$P(s_t, s_{t-1}, ..., s_1, s_0) = P(s_t / s_{t-1}) P(s_{t-1} / s_{t-2}) ... P(s_0) = P(s_0) \ prod \ [t=0..T-1] \ \{P(s_{t+1} / s_t)\}$$

As you can see, once we expand this, the expression becomes pretty lengthy but can be easily simplified with the use of the Markov property.

For instance, if we want to know if our baby will be calmer than upset today, or mathematically $P\ (calm_t\ /\ upset_t)$ we will have to take into consideration the previous days, as well. The maximum likelihood will be:

$$P\ (calm_t\ /\ upset_t)\ =\ count\ (calm_t\ /\ upset_t)\ /\ count\ (upset_{t-1})$$

But how often does (s1, s2, s3) occurs? And if it is not that frequent, how can we possible calculate P (s4 / s3, s2, s1)?

Of course, the more states we have the more accurate the probability will be. If the sequence does not happen, in that case, our maximum likelihood would be 0/0 or undefined.

That means that the general form, when the current state depends on all of the past states is rather hard to measure, since the probability distributions are not that easy to calculate.

Think of it this way. Suppose you are reading a book. You have read the first 499 words and you have to predict the 500th. Of course, this is not the greatest model since that set of 500 words is unique, meaning there is only one book with that exact order of 500 words. So, the probability, in this case, would be 1/1. Like I said, not the perfect model.

However, if you have only read the first word 'That' of the book and you want to predict the next one, the number of possible words that can appear after '*That*' is pretty much endless. So, what should you do? The best solution is to train on 3 or 4-word sequences, where the current word would depend on the previous 2 or 3 ones. Training with 3-state sequences is called a Markov model of a third order. Training with 2-state sequences is called a Markov model of a second order. We, however, are more interested in the trickier Markov models, which are the first-order Markov models, where the current state depends solely on one previous state.

Now, let's take the baby mood example from earlier. Suppose the baby can only go into three states: calm, upset, and asleep.

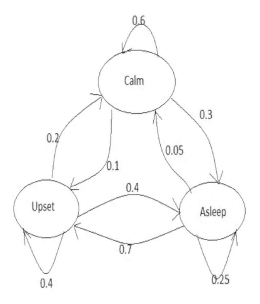

As you can see from the picture above, this is a perfect first-order Markov model example, since the probability, also referred to as *the weight*, depends solely on the current state, and it only affects the following state. That means that once the baby goes into another state, that state becomes the current state, the current state from before is what affected the current state that is now, which will eventually affect the state that the baby is about to go into.

Each of the three states: calm, upset, and asleep has 3 weights or probabilities, since the baby can not only go into one of the other two states, but it can also repeat the state that she is into.

The states and weights are represented by the M x M matrix of transition probability that is called *A*. *A* represents the probability of going from one state *x* to another state *y*.

$$A\ (x,y) = P\ (s_x\ /\ s_y)$$

or

$$A\ (x,y) = P\ (s_t) = x,\ s_{t-1} = y$$

Now, let's go back to our baby mood example. Since whenever the baby is in one state it has no other choice but to go to one of the three states, the sum of A (x) must be 1.

Calm → Calm = 0.6

Calm → Asleep = 0.3

Calm → Upset = 0.1

Asleep → Upset = 0.7

Asleep → Calm = 0.05

Asleep → Asleep = 0.25

Upset → Asleep = 0.4

Upset → Calm = 0.2

Upset → Upset = 0.4

In this definition, it is assumed that A is constant, but keep in mind that in reality this does not have to be the case. A doesn't have to be constant all time, it can also be a fraction of time, as well as depend on other factors. For instance, the probability of having an upset baby three days in a row may be higher when she is teething.

Another thing that you have to keep in mind, is the fact that it's also of great importance where you start modeling. If we start modeling an 'asleep' state, we have higher probability of transitioning to an 'upset' than 'calm' state. This is called *initial state distribution* and it is represented by and M-dimensional vector *Pxo*.

$Pxo\ (x) = P\ (S_o = y)$ *where* o – initial time index

Now that we know this, we can actually start tackling more specific questions. For instance, how can we calculate the probability of going from Calm → Calm → Upset → Asleep?

P (calm, calm, upset, asleep) = Pxo (calm) x P(calm / calm) x P (upset / calm) x P (asleep / upset)

Generally, all sequences can be calculated as:

$$Px(S_o) \, prod \, [t = 1.. \, T] \, \{P \, (s_t \, / \, s_{t-1})\}$$

Training a Markov Model

Let's try another example. Imagine that we want to train 3 sentences:

1. Tom likes pizza.
2. Tom likes burgers.
3. Tom loves cake.

If we treat each of the words as a different state, we have 6 different states: Tom, Likes, Pizza, Burgers, Loves, Cake.

If we decide to use the maximum likelihood we will have an initial state distribution that has 100 percent probability that the first word would be 'Tom', given the fact that no sentence starts with a different word.

That means that px0 [1,0,0,0,0,0] or px (Tom) = 1.

So, if the current word is 'Tom', then we have only 2 possibilities for 'likes' and 'loves'. P ('likes' / 'Tom') = 2/3. P ('loves' / 'Tom') = 1/3.

Then, P ('pizza' / 'likes') = P ('burgers' / 'likes') = ½.

P ('cake' / 'loves') = 1.

The other state probabilities equal 0.

This is great as an example, but you have to keep in mind that we have over a million different words. Even if we have tons of data we still may be unable to determine all of the possible sentences. For that reason, we use smoothed estimates and not maximum likelihood. We can achieve that by adding a small number to the numerator, naming it

epsilon, and then adding V*epsilon (V =
vocabulary size) to the denominator.

$$P (s_t = y \;/\; s_{t-1} = x) = [\text{count } (x \rightarrow y) + \text{epsilon}] \;/\; [\text{count } (x) + \text{epsilon}*V]$$

Markov Chains

Markov chains are those types of Markov models that represent random processes that happen over a certain period of time. Think of Markov models as a broad term, and Markov chains as the type of models we will be focusing on in this book. All of the previous examples were Markov chains, but in order for you to fully understand this concept, I will make things simple and present yet another great and easy-to-understand example.

Imagine a scenario where Burger 1 and Burger 2 are the only fast food companies in a country X. A fast food giant wants to tie up with one of those two companies, but is unsure about which one will be more profitable. So, the fast food giant hires a market research company in order to determine which one of these competitors will have a higher market share after let's say a month. At the time of hiring the research company, Burger 1 owns 55 % of the market share and Burger 2 owns 45 %.

This is what the market research company concludes:

P (B1 → B1) The probability of customers to stick with the brand Burger 1 over a month is 0.7

P (B1 →B2) The probability of customers to switch from Burger 1 to Burger 2 over a month is 0.3.

P (B2 → B2) The probability of customers to stick with Burger 2 for a month is 0.9.

P (B2 → B1) The probability that customers will switch from Burger 2 to Burger 1 over a month is 0.1.

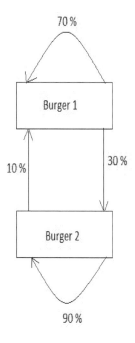

70 %

Burger 1

10 %

30 %

Burger 2

90 %

This is somewhat confusing since it shows how customers tend to stick with Burger 2 and Burger 2 has a lower market share. That means that this cannot be the greatest recommendation. Therefore, further transition calculations must be made.

For the sake of convenience, I will use these abbreviations in the following formulas:

MS (Market Share) and CMS (Current Market Share).

MS t+1 of Burger 1 = CMS of B1 x P (B1 → B1) + CMS of B2 x P(B2 → B1)

MS t+1 of Burger 2 = CMS of B2 x P(B2 → B2) + CMS of B1 x P(B1 → B2)

This can be done simply by looking at the matrix multiplication:

Current State x Transition Matrix = Final State

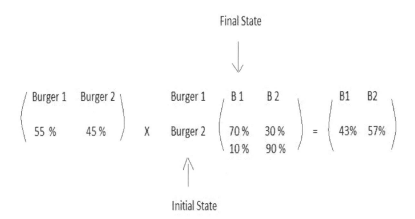

Final State

$$\begin{pmatrix} \text{Burger 1} & \text{Burger 2} \\ 55\% & 45\% \end{pmatrix} \times \begin{matrix} & \text{B 1} & \text{B 2} \\ \text{Burger 1} & & \\ \text{Burger 2} & 70\% & 30\% \\ & 10\% & 90\% \end{matrix} = \begin{pmatrix} \text{B1} & \text{B2} \\ 43\% & 57\% \end{pmatrix}$$

Initial State

As you can see from the picture above, Burger 1 may have a higher market share now but it will have a lower MS in a month. If we make the same calculations for two months:

Final State

↓

$$\begin{pmatrix} \text{Burger 1} & \text{Burger 2} \\ 43\% & 57\% \end{pmatrix} \times \begin{array}{c} \text{Burger 1} \\ \text{Burger 2} \end{array} \begin{pmatrix} \text{B 1} & \text{B 2} \\ 70\% & 30\% \\ 10\% & 90\% \end{pmatrix} = \begin{pmatrix} \text{B1} & \text{B2} \\ 36\% & 64\% \end{pmatrix}$$

↑

Initial State

Warming Up Python

In order for you to make predictions, you will need a lot more than the Markov model formulas. Sure, they work great if you are trying to determine what your partner's mood will be like tomorrow based on how they are feeling at the moment, but if you are looking for a way to predict some longer and much more complex sequences, then you will need a special tool to assist you. And what better way to make such complex calculations than with the greatest and most versatile programming language?

You don't need to write lengthy formulas on your wall nor spend days trying to predict something. Having basic Python programming skills is more than enough for you to master data science and decipher complex sequences in a matter of seconds.

However, in order for you to be able to make accurate prediction you will need something else besides decent programming skills and a good knowledge of Markov models. You will need to make sure that your Python is packed with the right equipment that will ensure efficient puzzle cracking.

The first and probably the most important thing you need to equip your Python with is **NymPy.** NymPy is a Python's library that comes with a huge collection of complex math functions that supports large and multi-dimensional matrices and arrays. Its amazing algebra is extremely useful for training Markov models since it provides random number capabilities and speedy, flawless operation.

If you want to operate on large and complex arrays, then it is probably the best idea to install the NymPy now. If you don't already have this super versatile library, go to the official Python site to install the most genuine version.

But, as important as it is, NymPy is not the only package that your Python should receive from you in order to help you on this data science journey. There are other packages that can support your complex operations and contribute to receiving more accurate results:

autocomplete - An autocomplete tool with an HMM model

cobe – Text generator, library, and chatbot that uses Markov Chains

gibi – A tool for creating random words with the help of Markov Chains

hmmlearn – HMMs with Scikit-learn

hmmus – HMM posterior decoding

marbl-python – Marbl implementation for presenting the Markov blankets in the Bayesian networks

Markov – HMM library

MarkovEquClasses – Algorithms for the Markov equivalence classes

Markovgen – A word generator based on the Markovian statistics

Markovgenerator – A Text generator based on the Markovian statistics

Markovify – A generator for semi-plausable sentences that are based on existing text

MCL_Markov_Cluster – An algorithm for implementing the Markov cluster

MCREPOGEN – Repository generator that is based on the Markovian statistics

mwordgen – A word generator based on the Markovian statistics

pyborg – An irc bot that replies to messages with the help of the Markov Chains

pydodo - A simple Markov Chain generator

pyEMMA – Emma's algorithms for Markov Models

PyMarkov - Markov Chains that are made easy

PyMarkovChain – Simple and easy Markov Chain implementation

PyMarkovTextGenerator – A text generator that is based on the Markov Chains

pythonic-porin – A package for reading data, visualization, etc, mostly for HMMs

treehmm - Tree-structured variational inference for Hidden Markov Models

twarkov - A tweet generator that is based on the Markovian statistics

twitter_markov - Creates Twitter accounts with Markov Chains

vokram – A toy implementation of the Markov Chains

Hidden Markov Models

With all of the previous examples predicting the next state was not that hard because the states could be directly observed. But what happens if the states are hidden and you cannot observe them?

Hidden Markov models are stochastic processes where the state cannot be directly observed. The only thing that can be observed is the output that is emitted by the unobservable states.

For instance, predicting a weather is easy. With the help of the formulas from before we can easily calculate the probability that tomorrow will be just as sunny as it is today. But how can we do it if we cannot actually see what the weather is like today?

Let's say that you want to know if it is raining or not, but you cannot see the weather nor hear the rain for that matter. You are a prisoner trapped in a prison cell. There are no windows and therefore you cannot directly observe the weather. The only thing you can observe is the guard's boots. If his boots are wet and dirty you assume that it is raining outside. If his boots are dry and clean, then there is no rain.

Intuition plays a big part of determining the unobservable states. And that may not be that hard. After all, we are all born with intuition. But building a model around that intuition? Now that is an entirely different thing. But don't despair. Just because they are hidden doesn't mean that they cannot be found. This chapter will teach you all about hidden Markov models and how to implement their algorithms in Python.

A Sales Funnel Example

You must have heard of the term 'sales funnel' before. The main idea behind this term is that customer interaction has different levels. People start as prospects and then transition to other states.

Prospects are most people. They are those that lurk but do not engage. Some of the prospects will end up browsing and even buying something occasionally, which transforms them into users. Those users that become pretty interested in whatever it is sold get engaged and become customer. However, since the customers usually don't buy a lot in a short period of time, they usually go back to being users. Some of the users that get disappointed may go back to being prospects, and so on. I believe I've made the transition cycle pretty clear and that you got the meaning that prospects, users, and customers are the three states that are dependent on each other.

Let's imagine for a second that we own an online store. Out of all the prospects that visit our site. 15 percent will actually sign up and only 5 percent will immediately become customers. Suppose that the users will cancel the account 5 percent of the time; 15 percent of the time users will buy something. Customers will cancel the accounts 2 percent of the time, and will go back to being users 95 percent of the time.

	Prospect	User	Customer
Prospect	0.80	0.15	0.05

User	0.05	0.80	0.15
Customer	0.02	0.95	0.03

This is a great way to observe how users behave and transition, but there is one giant problem with this particular model: we cannot determine the state of the users unless we ask each and every one of them. This is a typical hidden Markov model because the states here are hidden. Who says that users cannot visit our online store anonymously without us knowing? However, as long as we can observe the interactions and maybe learn about these transitions from other sources (for instance, think about Google Analytics), then we will have no problem solving the mystery.

But we cannot be sure when someone will transition from one state to another. The only thing we can observe is what the behavior of the users is. And as we know, for every behavior there is a given state.

Imagine that on our website we have five links that lead to five different pages: Home, Signup, Product, Checkout and Contact Us. Some of these pages may not be that important, such as Contact Us, but for example, Checkout may mean that a user has become a customer.

Now, suppose that we know the probabilities of these states:

	Prospect	User	Customer
Home	0.4	0.3	0.3

Signup	0.1	0.8	0.1
Product	0.1	0.3	0.6
Checkout	0	0.1	0.9
Contact Us	0.7	0.1	0.2

Now that we know the probability of the users transitioning to different states and the probability of their behavior when in a given state, we need to determine the probability that a user is in a certain state. In order to do this, we need to find out the probability that a user is in the customer state *P (Customer / S1, S2)*, as well the probability that a user is viewing the product page given that fact that they were customers multiplied by the signup probability *P (Product_Page / Customer) x P(Signup_Page / S2) x P (Homepage / S1).*

The problem here is the fact that there are a lot of things that we don't know and very few things that we do know. So, the best way is to rely on the Markov assumption and assume that the probability of going into a certain state depends solely on the current state. That means that instead of *P (Customer / S1, S2, ...Sn)* we should simplify to *P (Customer / Sn).*

The Components of HMM and Their Implementations

Hidden Markov models have three components:

1. <u>Evaluation</u>

Evaluation means being sure that the state is what generated the observe outcome. And since the state is hidden we cannot be absolutely sure in this. Our job here is to determine the likelihood that our model was actually the one that created the sequence we are now modeling. This is also super useful for determining, for instance, if Home - - > Signup is more probable than say Product - - > Checkout.

The evaluation can be performed by using the well-known Hmm algorithm – *The Forward - Backward Algorithm.* This algorithm represents the probability that an emission will happen as a result of its underlying states, or $P(e_k / s)$. This is proportional to the joint e_k distribution: $P(e_k / s) \propto P(e_k, s)$. This can be split into:

$$P(S_{k+1}, S_{k+2}, ... Sn / e_k, S1, S2, ..., S_k) \, P(e_k, S1, S2, ..., S_k)$$

meaning

$$P(e_k / s) \propto P(S_{k+1}, S_{k+2}, ... Sn / e_k,) \, P(e_k, S1, S2, ..., S_k)$$

Graphically, we can present the Forward-Backward algorithm this way:

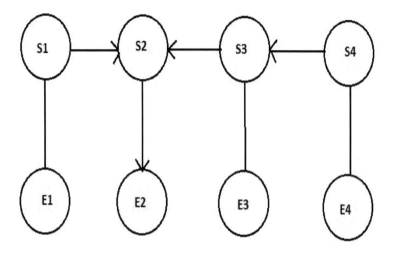

Now, using the example from earlier, let's just calculate the probability of this sequence: Home - -> Signup - - > Product - -> Checkout. But before all else, we must first create a Forward-Backward class:

```
class ForwardBackward:
    def __init__():
```

```python
        self.observations              =
['homepage',  'signup',  'product',
'checkout']
        self.states    =    ['Prospect',
'User', 'Customer']
        self.emissions = ['homepage',
'signup',        'product        page',
'checkout',\
                          'contact
us']


        self.start_probability = {
            'Prospect': 0.8,
            'User': 0.15,
            'Customer': 0.05
        }


        self.transition_probability    =
np.array([
            [0.8, 0.15, 0.05],
            [0.05, 0.80, 0.15],
```

```python
        [0.02, 0.95, 0.03]
    ])

    self.emission_probability      =
np.array([
        [0.4, 0.3, 0.3], # homepage
        [0.1, 0.8, 0.1], # signup
        [0.1,  0.3,  0.6], #  product
page
        [0, 0.1, 0.9],  # checkout
        [0.7, 0.1, 0.2] # contact us
    ])

    self.end_state = 'Ending'
```

Now that we have imported the transition matrix, and the probabilities for the emissions, let's define the forward step:

```python
class ForwardBackward:
    # __init__
```

```python
def forward():
  forward = []
  f_previous = {}

  for(i          in          xrange(1,
len(self.observations))):
    f_curr = {}
    for(state in self.states):
      if i == 0:
        prev_f_sum                  =
self.start_probability[state]
      else:
        prev_f_sum = 0.0
        for (k in self.states):
          prev_f_sum              +=
f_previous.get(k, 0.0) * \

self.transition_probability[k][sta
te]
```

```
            f_curr[state]              =
self.emission_probability[state][s
elf.observations[i]]
            f_curr[state]              =
f_curr[state] * prev_f_sum
            forward.append(f_curr)
            f_previous = f_curr


    p_fwd = 0.0
    for(k in self.states):
        p_fwd += f_previous[k] *
self.transition_probability[k][sel
f.end_state]


    {'probability':            p_fwd,
'sequence': forward}
```

Now, let's just define the backward algorithm:

```
class ForwardBackward:
    # __init__
```

```
# forward
def backward():
  backward = []
  b_prev = {}

  for(i                                in
xrange(len(self.observations),   0,
-1)):
      b_curr = {}
      for(state in self.states):
        if i == 0:
          b_curr[state]              =
self.transition_probability[state]
[self.end_state]
        else:
          sum = 0.0
          for (k in self.states):
            sum                      +=
self.transition_probability[state]
[k] * \
```

```
self.emission_probability[k][self.
observations[x_plus]] * \
            b_prev[k]
        backward.insert(0, b_curr)
        b_prev = b_curr

    p_bkw = 0.0

    for (s in self.states):
        sum                        +=
self.start_probability[s] * \

self.emission_probability[s][self.
observations[0]] * \
            b_prev[s]

    {'probability':               p_bkw,
'sequence': backward}
```

Now we must try these two together and state that they are the same since otherwise this will all turn out to be wrong:

```
class ForwardBackward:
    # __init__
    # forward
    # backward

    def forward_backward():
        size = len(self.observations)
        forward = forward()
        backward = backward()

        posterior = {}
        for(s in self.states):
            posterior[s] = []
            for (i in xrange(1, size)):
                value                          =
forward['sequence'][i][s] * \
```

```
      backward['sequence'][i][s]
/ forward['probability'])
      posterior[s].append()


      return    [forward,    backward,
posterior]
```

(1)

2. <u>Decoding</u>

Decoding is probably easiest to explain since it is the most straightforward of the three HMM components. What is the best path of states based on what we can actually observe?

Mathematically this will be $\pi * = \arg \max \pi\ P(x, \pi)$. Here, π is the state vector and x represents the observations.

This can be achieved with the help of the Viterbi algorithm which graphically looks like this:

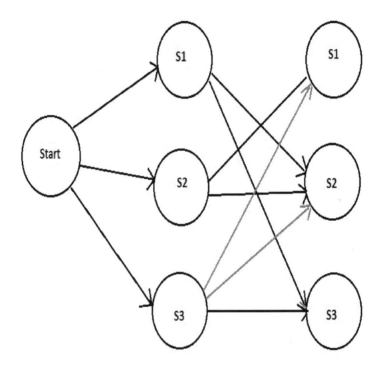

This algorithm's main job is to cross a set of states in the best way possible. Here is the Python implementation for this algorithm:

```
def viterbi(obs, states, start_p, trans_p, emit_p):
```

```
V = [{}]
for st in states:
    V[0][st]     =     {"prob":
start_p[st] * emit_p[st][obs[0]],
"prev": None}
# When t is larger than 0,
run Viterbi
    for t in range(1, len(obs)):
        V.append({})
        for st in states:
            max_tr_prob      =
max(V[t-
1][prev_st]["prob"]*trans_p[prev_s
t][st] for prev_st in states)
            for    prev_st    in
states:
                if          V[t-
1][prev_st]["prob"]           *
trans_p[prev_st][st]          ==
max_tr_prob:
```

```python
                    max_prob       =
max_tr_prob * emit_p[st][obs[t]]
                    V[t][st]       =
{"prob":       max_prob,       "prev":
prev_st}
                    break
    for line in dptable(V):
        print line
    opt = []
    # The highest probability
    max_prob = max(value["prob"]
for value in V[-1].values())
    previous = None
    # Get the most likely state,
as well as its backtract
    for    st,    data    in    V[-
1].items():
        if    data["prob"]      ==
max_prob:
            opt.append(st)
            previous = st
```

```python
            break
        # Following the backtract
until the 1st observation
        for t in range(len(V) - 2, -
1, -1):
            opt.insert(0,    V[t    +
1][previous]["prev"])
            previous     =    V[t    +
1][previous]["prev"]


    print 'The  steps  of  states
are ' + ' '.join(opt) + ' with
highest  probability  of  %s'  %
max_prob


  def dptable(V):
        # Print the table of steps
from dictionary
        yield " ".join(("%12d" % i)
for i in range(len(V)))
        for state in V[0]:
```

```
yield "%.7s: " % state +
"    ".join("%.7s" % ("%f" %
v[state]["prob"]) for v in V)
```

(2)

3. <u>Learning</u>

The learning problem seems like an easy one. Once you have your observations and state sequences, what is most probable to happen next?

And while there isn't really enough accessible data when it comes to the behaviors of the users given the views of the page, you can solve the learning problem by implementing the *Baum-Welch algorithm*.

The next code is somewhat longer that the previous ones, but once you implement it in Python you will see that it works flawlessly.

```python
from   numpy.random.mtrand   import
dirichlet
from numpy import *
from sys import *

numstates = 5
alphabet = 5
ll_bound = 10.0

if len(argv) != 3:
    print      "required      input:
trainfile testfile"
    assert(False)

train_file = argv[1]
test_file = argv[2]

def number(num):
    return float(num)
```

```python
# Normalize the values. They
should sum to 1.0
def normalize(arr):
  sumarr = number(sum(arr))
  if sumarr != 0.0:
      for i in range(len(arr)):
          arr[i] = arr[i] / sumarr


# A probable and finite automaton
model's state (I,F,S,T)
# I - an array of the initial
state probabilities
# F - an array of all of the final
probabilities of the states
# S - the matrix of the symbols
probabilities of the states
# T - the 3d matrix of the
transition probabilities


# The creation of a 0-probability
model
```

```python
def
emptymodel(numstates,alphabet):
    I   =   array([number(0.0)]   *
numstates)
    F   =   array([number(0.0)]   *
numstates)
    S = []
    for i in range(numstates):
        newrow =  array([number(0.0)]
* alphabet)
        S.append(newrow)

    T = []
    for i in range(alphabet):
        T.append([])
        for j in range(numstates):
            newrow                =
array([number(0.0)] * numstates)
            T[i].append(newrow)

    return (I,F,S,T)
```

```python
# The creation of a fully
connected model with random
probabilities
def randommodel(numstates,
alphabet):
    I = array(dirichlet([1] *
numstates))
    F = array([0.0] * numstates)
    S = []
    # here F is the end of the
string symbol
    for i in range(numstates):
        probs = dirichlet([1] *
(alphabet + 1))
        newrow =
array(probs[0:alphabet])
        normalize(newrow)
        S.append(newrow)
        F[i] = probs[alphabet]
```

```
T = []
for i in range(alphabet):
    T.append([])
    for j in range(numstates):
        newrow                  =
array(dirichlet([1] * numstates))
        T[i].append(newrow)


return (I,F,S,T)


# The calculation of the string
probabilities with recursion
def
computeprobabilityrecursion((I,F,S
,T),sequence,index,state,DPdict):
    # Probability = P (final)
    if index == len(sequence):
        DPdict[tuple([state])]      =
F[state]
        return F[state]
```

```python
    # Return the hashed result
    if  DPdict.has_key(tuple([state]
+ sequence[index:len(sequence)]])):
        return  DPdict[tuple([state]
+ sequence[index:len(sequence)]])]


    # For   every   next   state   s
possible:
    # Probability  =  P(symbol)  *
P(transition to s) * P(future)
    symb_prob                    =
S[state][sequence[index]]
    final_prob = F[state]
    prob  = number(0.0)
    for          nextstate         in
range(len(T[sequence[index]][state
])):
        if
T[sequence[index]][state][nextstat
e] > 0.0:
```

```
        trans_prob            =
T[sequence[index]][state][nextstat
e]
        future_prob           =
computeprobabilityrecursion((I,F,S
,T),sequence,index+1,nextstate,DPd
ict)
        prob    =    prob    +
(number(1.0)-final_prob)         *
symb_prob    *    trans_prob    *
future_prob

    # Hash the result
    DPdict[tuple([state]        +
sequence[index:len(sequence)])]   =
prob
    return prob

# The calculation of the string
probabilities    forwards    using
recursion
```

```python
def
computeprobability((I,F,S,T),seque
nce,DPdict):
    result = number(0.0)

    for state in range(len(I)):
        if I[state] > 0.0:
            result   =   result   +
I[state]                          *
computeprobabilityrecursion((I,F,S
,T),sequence,0,state,DPdict)
    return result


# This  calculates   all   of   the
probabilities   from   a   list   of
examples
def
computeprobabilities((I,F,S,T),set
t):
  probs = []
  DPdict = dict()
```

```
    for sequence in sett:

probs.append(computeprobability((I
,F,S,T),sequence,DPdict))
    return probs


# This calculates the string
probabilities backward with
recursion
def
computeprobabilityrecursionreverse
((I,F,S,T),sequence,index,state,DP
dict):
    # Probability = P(initial)
    if index == 0:
        DPdict[tuple([state])]        =
I[state]
        return I[state]

    # Return the hashed result
```

```python
    if  DPdict.has_key(tuple([state]
+ sequence[0:index])):
        return  DPdict[tuple([state]
+ sequence[0:index])]


    # For  every  possible  previous
state s:
    # Probability  +=  P(symbol)  *
P(transition from s) * P(past)
    prob = number(0.0)
    for prevstate in range(len(I)):
        if         T[sequence[index-
1]][prevstate][state] > 0.0:
            final_prob            =
F[prevstate]
            symb_prob             =
S[prevstate][sequence[index-1]]
            trans_prob            =
T[sequence[index-
1]][prevstate][state]
```

```python
        past_prob                 =
computeprobabilityrecursionreverse
((I,F,S,T),sequence,index-
1,prevstate,DPdict)

        prob      =      prob      +
((number(1.0)-final_prob)            *
symb_prob      *      trans_prob      *
past_prob)

    # Hash the result
    DPdict[tuple([state]              +
sequence[0:index])] = prob
    return prob

#      This      computes      string
probabilities    backwards    with    a
recursion
def
computeprobabilityreverse((I,F,S,T
),sequence,DPdict):
```

```
    result = number(0.0)

    # For every final state f:
    # Probability += P(end in f) *
P(past)
    for state in range(len(I)):
        result = result + F[state] *
computeprobabilityrecursionreverse
((I,F,S,T),sequence,len(sequence),
state,DPdict)
    return result


# This computes all of the
probabilities from a list of
examples
def
computeprobabilitiesreverse((I,F,S
,T),sett):
  probs = []
  DPdict = dict()
  for sequence in sett:
```

```python
    probs.append(computeprobabilityrev
    erse((I,F,S,T),sequence,DPdict))
     return probs

def iterateEM((I,F,S,T),sett):
    backward = dict()
    probs = []
    for sequence in sett:

probs.append(computeprobability((I
,F,S,T),sequence,backward))
        # backward = P(s|start(q))

    forward = dict()
    for sequence in sett:

computeprobabilityreverse((I,F,S,T
),sequence,forward)
        # forward = P(s,end(q))
```

```python
    (Inew,Fnew,Snew,Tnew)                =
emptymodel(numstates,alphabet)

    # P(I(q)|s) =   P(I(q),s)/P(s)
    #             P(I(q)|s)              =
P(I(q))*P(s|start(q))/P(s)
    for state in range(len(I)):
        for seq in range(len(sett)):
            sequence = sett[seq]
            prob = probs[seq]
            key   =  tuple([state]    +
sequence)
            if backward.has_key(key):
                Inew[state]            =
Inew[state]    +    ((I[state]      *
backward[key]) / prob)
    normalize(Inew)

    # P(F(q)|s) =   P(F(q),s)/P(s)
    #             P(F(q)|s)              =
P(end(q),s)*P(F(q))/P(s)
```

```
for state in range(len(I)):
    for seq in range(len(sett)):
        sequence = sett[seq]
        prob = probs[seq]
        key    =   tuple([state]   +
sequence)
        if forward.has_key(key):
            Fnew[state]            =
Fnew[state]    +    ((F[state]    *
forward[key]) / prob)



    #            P(S(q,a)|s)          =
P(S(q,a),s)/P(s)
    #            P(S(q,a)|s)          =
P(end(q),S(q,a),tail(q))/P(s)
    #            P(S(q,a)|s)          =
P(end(q),head(s))*P(tail(s)|start(
q))/P(s)
    Stotal = number(0.0)
    for seq in range(len(sett)):
```

```python
        sequence = sett[seq]
        prob = probs[seq]
        for           index           in
range(len(sequence)):
            key = tuple([state] +
sequence[0:index])
            if
forward.has_key(key):
                key2              =
tuple([state]                      +
sequence[index:len(sequence)])
                if
backward.has_key(key2):
                    symprob        =
forward[key] * backward[key2]

Snew[state][sequence[index]]        =
Snew[state][sequence[index]]        +
(symprob / prob)

        if Fnew[state] != 0.0:
```

```
        Fnew[state] = Fnew[state]
/ (Fnew[state] + sum(Snew[state]))
      normalize(Snew[state])


  for state in range(len(I)):
     for seq in range(len(sett)):
         sequence = sett[seq]
         prob = probs[seq]
         for        index        in
range(len(sequence)):
            key1 = tuple([state] +
sequence[0:index])
            if
forward.has_key(key1):
               for    state2    in
range(len(I)):
                  key2           =
tuple([state2]            +
sequence[(index+1):len(sequence)])
                  if
backward.has_key(key2):
```

```
                    transprob   =
(number(1.0)    -       F[state])       *
S[state][sequence[index]]               *
T[sequence[index]][state][state2]
                    transprob   =
forward[key1]       *       transprob   *
backward[key2]


Tnew[sequence[index]][state][state
2]                                      =
Tnew[sequence[index]][state][state
2] + (transprob / prob)

    for a in range(alphabet):
        for state in range(len(I)):
            normalize(Tnew[a][state])


    return (Inew,Fnew,Snew,Tnew)

def loglikelihood(probs):
    sumt = number(0.0)
```

```python
    log2 = log10(number(2.0))
    for index in range(len(probs)):
        term = log10(probs[index])
/ log2
        sumt = sumt + term
    return sumt


def readset(f):
 sett = []
 line = f.readline()
 l = line.split(" ")
 num_strings = int(l[0])
 alphabet_size = int(l[1])
 for n in range(num_strings):
     line = f.readline()
     l = line.split(" ")
     sett = sett + [[int(i) for i
in l[1:len(l)]]]
  return alphabet_size, sett


def writeprobs(probs,f):
```

```python
    f.write(str(len(probs)) + "\n")
    for i in range(len(probs)):
        f.write(str(probs[i]) + "\n")


alphabet, train =
readset(open(train_file,"r"))
alphabet, test =
readset(open(test_file,"r"))

model =
randommodel(numstates,alphabet)
print "loglikelihood:",
loglikelihood(computeprobabilities
(model,train+test))

prev = -1.0
ll = -1.0
while prev == -1.0 or ll - prev >
ll_bound:
    prev = ll
```

```
    m                         =
iterateEM(model,train+test)
    probs                     =
computeprobabilities(m,train+test)
    ll = loglikelihood(probs)
    print "loglikelihood:", ll
    model = m

writeprobs(computeprobabilities(m,
test),open(test_file+".bm","w"))
```

(3)

Building and Training an HMM

Building and training a Hidden Markov model is actually a lot easier than you think, and this chapter will prove that to you.

First, let's start with the available models:

hmm.GaussianHMM – HMM with Gaussian emissions
hmm.GMMHMM – HMM with Gaussian mixture emissions
hmm.MultinomialHMM – HMM with multinomial emissions

Pass the parametres to the constructor, and call `sample` to generate the samples. Here is how:

```
>>> import numpy as np
```

```
>>> from hmmlearn import hmm
>>> np.random.seed(42)

>>> model =
hmm.GaussianHMM(n_components=3,
covariance_type="full")
>>> model.startprob_ =
np.array([0.6, 0.3, 0.1])
>>> model.transmat_ =
np.array([[0.7, 0.2, 0.1],
... 
[0.3, 0.5, 0.2],
...
[0.3, 0.3, 0.4]])
>>> model.means_ = np.array([[0.0,
0.0], [3.0, -3.0], [5.0, 10.0]])
>>> model.covars_ =
np.tile(np.identity(2), (3, 1, 1))
>>> X, Z = model.sample(100)
```

Know that there is no need for the transition probability matrix to be automatic. Simply define the left-right Hidden Markov model like this:

```
>>>                    lr                =
hmm.GaussianHMM(n_components=3,
covariance_type="diag",
...
init_params="cm", params="cmt")
>>> lr.startprob_ = np.array([1.0,
0.0, 0.0])
>>> lr.transmat_ = np.array([[0.5,
0.5, 0.0],
...                             [0.0,
0.5, 0.5],
...                             [0.0,
0.0, 1.0]])
```

Fixing Parameters

Should the need for fixing the parameters arise, don't worry. Each of the HMM parameters have a character code that can help with customization the initialization. Just know that the EM algorithm must have a starting point in order to proceed, so make sure to provide one explicitly:

1. Make sure that the character code is missing from init_params
2. Set the parameter to the value you desire

For instance, let's consider this HMM with a transition matrix that is explicitly initialized:

```
>>> model = hmm.GaussianHMM(n_components=3, n_iter=100, init_params="mcs")
```

```
>>>          model.transmat_           =
np.array([[0.7, 0.2, 0.1],
...
[0.3, 0.5, 0.2],
...
[0.3, 0.3, 0.4]])
```

In order for you to fix parameters as some specific values you will have to remove the character from `params` first, and then make sure that the value is set before the actual training.

Training

To train an HMM, call the `fit` method. The input will be a matrix of samples and sequence lengths. Just make sure that you run fit with as many initializations as possible, and then choose the model with the highest score.

To obtain the optimal hidden states you can call the `predict` method, which can be specified with a decoder algorithm. The best choice is the Viterbi algorithm.

The input will be a single sequence of the values that were observed. The state in `remodel` will be different than the ones in the generating model.

```
>>> remodel =
hmm.GaussianHMM(n_components=3,
covariance_type="full",
n_iter=100)
>>> remodel.fit(X)
GaussianHMM(algorithm='viterbi',...
.
>>> Z2 = remodel.predict(X)
```

Keep in mind that the convergence in the step number may or may not happen, depending on the data.

To diagnose the convergence, use `monitor`.

```
>>> remodel.monitor_
ConvergenceMonitor(history=[...],
          iter=12,        n_iter=100,
tol=0.01, verbose=False)
>>> remodel.monitor_.converged
True
```

All of the previous examples used single sequence observation. Working with multiple sequences is a bit more complicated.

Let's take these two sequences into consideration:
```
>>> X1 = [[0.5], [1.0], [-1.0],
[0.42], [0.24]]
```

```
>>> X2 = [[2.4], [4.2], [0.5], [-
0.24]]
```

In order to pass them into `fit` and `predict`, we first have to make sure that they are in a single array, and then to calculate the array of the lengths of the sequences.

```
>>> X = np.concatenate([X1, X2])
>>> lengths = [len(X1), len(X2)]
```

At the end, simply call the method with X and `lengths`.

```
>>>
hmm.GaussianHMM(n_components=3).fi
t(X, lengths)
GaussianHMM(algorithm='viterbi',
...
```

Saving the HMM

After training, obviously you would want to save your Hidden Markov model. You can save it for future use with the `pickle` module or in the `joblib` package.

```
>>> from sklearn.externals import joblib
>>> joblib.dump(remodel, "filename.pkl")
["filename.pkl"]
>>> joblib.load("filename.pkl")
GaussianHMM(algorithm='viterbi',...
.
(4)
```

Part of Speech Tagging

As our first real-world application, we will build a part-of-speech tagger. We all know how the English language has nouns, verbs, adjectives, etc., and we can all easily tag the parts of speech in a sentence. But how can we create and train an algorithm to do so?

For that purpose, we will mostly rely on the Viterbi Algorithm and the Brown Corpus – the very first electronic corpus. It is packed with more than a million words along with parts of speech, but all of them are normal tags.

Our approach for building a speech tagger has 2 classes:

CorpusPaser – In charge for parsing the Brown Corpus

POSTagger – In charge for tagging new data based on the corpus training data

The main thing when it comes to building the part-of-speech tagger is to feed proper data. However, first, we need to make our initial test where we will store each of the transitions from a combination of word tags in an array of 2, and then wrap it in a class called CorpusParser::TagWorld.

```
import unittest

class
CorpusParserTest(unittest.TestCase
):
    def setUp():
        self.stream    =    "\tSeveral/ap
defendants/nns ./.\n"
        self.blank = "\t   \n"
```

```
def it_parses_a_line(self):
    cp = CorpusParser()
    null = cp.TagWord(word =
"START", tag = "START")
    several = cp.TagWord(word =
"Several", tag = "ap")
    defendants = cp.TagWord(word =
"defendants", tag = "nns")
    period = cp.TagWord(word =
".", tag =".")

    expectations = [
        [null, several],
        [several, defendants],
        [defendants, period]
    ]

    for (token in
cp.parse(self.stream)):
        self.assertEqual(token,
expectations.pop(0))
```

```
self.assertEqual(len(expectations)
, 0)

    def
it_doesnt_allow_blank_lines(self):
        cp = CorpusParser()

        for(token                        in
cp.parse(self.blank)):
            raise        Exception("Should
never happen")
```

The code checks if two cases are parsed the right way. The first case is concerned with parsing stream into tokens, and the other one is a simple check to see if the blank lines (which Brown Corpus is filled with) are actually being avoided.

Initially, we would have a code like this one:

```
class CorpusParser:
  NULL_CHARACTER = "START"
  STOP = "\n"
  SPLITTER = "/"

  class TagWord:
    def __init__(self, **kwargs):
      setattr(self,          'word',
kwargs['word'])
      setattr(self,           'tag',
kwargs['tag'])

  def __init__(self):
    self.ngram = 2

  def __iter__(self):
    return self

  def next(self):
```

```
char = self.file.read(1)

if self.stop_iteration: raise
StopIteration

if not char and self.pos != ''
and self.word != '':
    self.ngrams.pop(0)

self.ngrams.append(TagWord(word =
self.word, tag = self.tag))
    self.stop_iteration = True
    return self.ngrams

if char == "\t" or (self.word
== "" && STOP.contains(char)):
    return None
elif char == SPLITTER:
    self.parse_word = false
elif STOP.contains(char):
    self.ngrams.pop(0)
```

```python
        self.ngrams.append(TagWord(word =
self.word, tag = self.pos))

            self.word = ''
            self.pos = ''
            self.parse_word = True

            return self.ngrams
        elif self.parse_word:
            self.word += char
        else:
            self.pos += char

    def parse(file):
        self.ngrams = [
            TagWord(NULL_CHARACTER,
NULL_CHARACTER),
            TagWord(NULL_CHARACTER,
NULL_CHARACTER)
        ]
```

```
self.word = ''
self.pos = ''
self.parse_word = True
self.file = file


return self
```

Now we are ready to actually write our part of speech tagger:

1. First, we take data from CorpusParser
2. Then we store it internally in order to calculate the combinations of word tags.
3. We do the same for the tag transitions.

Using maximum likelihood, we now check the probability of a tag based on its previous tag. We state that the probability equals the count of the two tags divided by the previous tag's count:

```python
from collections import
defaultdict
class POSTagger:
  def __init__(self, data_io):
    self.corpus_parser                =
CorpusParser()
    self.data_io = data_io
    self.trained = False

  def train():
    if not self.trained:
      self.tags = set(["Start"])
      self.tag_combos                =
defaultdict(lambda: 0, {})
      self.tag_frequencies           =
defaultdict(lambda: 0, {})
      self.word_tag_combos           =
defaultdict(lambda: 0, {})

      for(io in self.data_io):
```

```python
        for(line                    in
io.readlines()):
            for(ngram               in
self.corpus_parser.parse(line)):
            write(ngram)
        self.trained = True


    def write(ngram):
        if ngram[0].tag == 'START':

self.tag_frequencies['START'] += 1

self.word_tag_combos['START/START'
] += 1

        self.tags.append(ngram[-
1].tag)
        self.tag_frequencies[ngram[-
1].tag] += 1
```

```python
        self.word_tag_combos["/".join([ngr
am[-1].word, ngram[-1].tag])] += 1

        self.tag_combos["/".join([ngram[0]
.tag, ngram[-1].tag])] += 1

    def
tag_probability(previous_tag,
current_tag):
        denom                            =
self.tag_frequencies[previous_tag]

        if denom == 0:
            0.0
        else:

self.tag_combos["/".join(previous_
tag, current_tag)] / float(denom)
```

Now, we need to address the word tag combos'
probability. We do it by introducing this:

```python
import StringIO
class
TestPOSTagger(unittest.TestCase):
  def setUp():
    self.stream    =    StringIO("A/B
C/D C/D A/D A/B ./.")
    self.pos_tagger                     =
POSTagger([StringIO.StringIO(self.
stream)])
    self.pos_tagger.train()

  def
it_calculates_probability_of_word_
and_tag(self):

self.assertEqual(self.pos_tagger.w
ord_tag_probability("Z", "Z"), 0)
```

```python
# A and B happens 2 times,
count of b happens twice therefore
100%

self.assertEqual(self.pos_tagger.w
ord_tag_probability("A", "B"), 1)

# A and D happens 1 time,
count of D happens 3 times so 1/3

self.assertEqual(self.pos_tagger.w
ord_tag_probability("A",     "D"),
1.0/3.0)

# START and START happens 1,
time, count of start happens 1 so
1

self.assertEqual(self.pos_tagger.w
ord_tag_probability("START",
"START"), 1)
```

```
self.assertEqual(self.pos_tagger.w
ord_tag_probability(".", "."), 1)
```

To make sure that will actually work in the POSTTagger, we write this:

```
class POSTagger:
    # __init__
    # train
    # write
    # tag_probability

    def    word_tag_probability(word,
tag):
    denom                           =
self.tag_frequencies[tag]

        if denom == 0:
        0.0
```

```
    else:

self.word_tag_combos["/".join(word
, tag)] / float(denom)
```

And now, we are able to ask ourselves how probable is a tag sequence given a certain word. That means the probability of the current tag that depends on the previous tag, multiplied by the word. This is the code:

```
class
TestPOSTagger(unittest.TestCase):
    # setUp
    #
it_calculates_probability_of_word_
and_tag

    def
it_calculates_probability_of_words
_and_tags(self):
```

```python
    words = ['START', 'A', 'C',
'A', 'A', '.']
    tags           = ['START',
'B','D','D','B','.']
    tagger = self.pos_tagger

    tag_probabilities   =   reduce(
(lambda x, y: x * y), [
        tagger.tag_probability("B",
"D"),
        tagger.tag_probability("D",
"D"),
        tagger.tag_probability("D",
"B"),
        tagger.tag_probability("B",
".")
    ])

    word_probabilities   =   reduce(
(lambda x, y: x * y), [
```

```python
    tagger.word_tag_probability("A",
"B"),  # 1

    tagger.word_tag_probability("C",
"D"),

    tagger.word_tag_probability("A",
"D"),

    tagger.word_tag_probability("A",
"B"),  # 1
    ])

    expected  =  word_probabilities
* tag_probabilities

self.assertEqual(tagger.probabilit
y_of_word_tag(words,tags),
expected)
```

Let's implement this in the POSTagger:

```python
class POSTagger:
    # __init__
    # train
    # write
    # tag_probability
    # word_tag_probability
    def probability_of_word_tag(word_sequence, tag_sequence):
        if len(word_sequence) != len(tag_sequence):
            raise Exception('The word and tags must be the same length!')

        length = len(word_sequence)

        probability = 1.0
```

```python
    for (i in xrange(1, length)):
        probability *= (

tag_probability(tag_sequence[i   -
1], tag_sequence[i]) *

word_tag_probability(word_sequence
[i], tag_sequence[i])
            )

    Probability
```

Let's write a small test that will determine the optimal sequence of tags, now that we know the sentence and the training data:

```python
class
TestPOSTagger(unittest.TestCase):
    # setUp
```

```
    #
it_calculates_probability_of_word_
and_tag
    #
it_calculates_probability_of_words
_and_tags(self):
  def viterbi(self):
    training = "I/PRO want/V to/TO
race/V ./. I/PRO like/V cats/N
./."
    sentence = 'I want to race.'
    tagger = self.pos_tagger
    expected = ['START', 'PRO',
'V', 'TO', 'V', '.']

self.assertEqual(pos_tagger.viterb
i(sentence), expected)
```

We now use the Viterbi algorithm:

```python
class POSTagger:
    #__init__
    # train
    # write
    # tag_probability
    # word_tag_probability
    # probability_of_word_tag

    def viterbi(sentence):
        # parts
        last_viterbi = {}
        backpointers = ["START"]

    for (tag in self.tags):
        if tag == 'START':
            next()
        else:
            probability                        =
tag_probability('START', tag) * \
```

```python
word_tag_probability(parts[0],
tag)

        if probability > 0:
            last_viterbi[tag]          =
probability

        backpointers.append(
            max(v        for        v        in
last_viterbi.itervalues()) or
            max(v        for        v        in
self.tag_frequencies.itervalues())
        )
```

Now we just iterate through the rest:

```python
class POSTagger:
    #__init__
    # train
    # write
```

```python
# tag_probability
# word_tag_probability
# probability_of_word_tag

def viterbi(sentence):
  # parts
  # initialization
  for(part in parts[1:]):
    viterbi = {}
    for(tag in self.tags):
      if tag == 'START':
        next()

      if last_viterbi:
        break

      best_previous = max(
        for((prev_tag,
probability)                               in
last_viterbi.iteritems()):
          probability * \
```

```
tag_probability(prev_tag, tag) * \

word_tag_probability(part,tag)
        )
        best_tag                    =
best_previous[0]

        probability                 =
last_viterbi[best_tag] * \
        tag_probability(best_tag,
tag) * \
        word_tag_probability(part,
tag)

        if probability > 0:
            viterbi[tag]            =
probability


        last_viterbi = viterbi
```

```
        backpointers << (
            max(v        for        v        in
last_viterbi.itervalues())  or
            max(v        for        v        in
self.tag_frequencies.itervalues())
            )

        backpointers
```

It is essential to write a cross-validation test now, so we can see at least 20 percent of accuracy, since the model is naive.

```
class
CrossValidationTest(unittest.TestC
ase):
    def setUp(self):
        self.files                    =
Glob('./data/brown/c***')
```

```python
FOLDS = 10


def cross_validate(self):
  for (i in xrange(0,FOLDS)):
    splits = len(self.files) /
FOLDS
    self.validation_indexes =
range(i * splits, (i + 1) *
splits)
    self.training_indexes =
range(0, len(self.files)) -
self.validation_indexes
    self.validation_files =
(file for idx, file in
enumerate(self.files))
    self.training_files = (file
for idx, file in
enumerate(self.files))

    validate(fold)
```

```python
    def validate(self, fold):
      pos_tagger                    =
POSTagger.from_filepaths(training_
files, true)

      misses = 0
      successes = 0

      for(vf                         in
self.validation_files):
         with open(vf,'rb') as f:
            for(l in f.readlines()):
               if re.match(r"\A\s+\z/",
l):
                  next()
               else:
                  words = []
                  parts_of_speech     =
['START']
                  for     (ppp      in
re.split(r"\s+")):
```

```
            z   =   re.split(r"\/",
ppp)
                words.append(z[0])

parts_of_speech.append(z[1])

            tag_seq                 =
pos_tagger.viterbi("
".join(words))
            for        (k,v)       in
zip(tag_seq, parts_of_speech))
                misses += sum((k !=
v) ? 1 : 0
            for        (k,v)       in
zip(tag_seq, parts_of_speech))
                successes += sum((k
== v) ? 1 : 0

    print "Error  rate  was:  "  +
float(misses) / float(successes +
misses)
```

The error rate here is about 20-30 percent, which obviously, is not ideal. The best way to make the model better is to forget looking back one word at a time so you can determine the probability of a tag based on the previous two tags.

This example really works well, but not only for speech tagging. You can easily use this example and the way we have built this code to create a user state model – the example that we talked about earlier.

(5)

Random Text Generator

Another interesting application of the Markov models is to create a code that will generate random text with the help of given corpus. Sure, you can take random words and drop them all in one pool, but that will most likely result in a meaningless and unreadable text.

The algorithm is the following:

1. Take two sequential words form the corpus. We are about to create a chain where the last 2 words will represent the chain's current state.
2. Check the corpus and see if the current state (meaning the last 2 words) occur more than once. If they do, choose one of them randomly, and then add the word that comes after them at the end of

that chain. That way you update the current state.

3. Keep repeating step 2 until you are sure that you have reached the preferable length of the generated text.

Make sure that when you read and split your corpus to words you will not remove the commas and other punctuation signs. That way the text will remain realistic.

For this application, we will use one simple and short example. This is our text:

A is the father of B.
C is the father of A.

Now, using the algorithm from before, we will build our dictionary:

{('A', 'is'): ['the'],

('B.', 'C'): ['is'],
('C', 'is'): ['the'],
('father', 'of'): ['B.', 'A.'],
('is', 'the'): ['father', 'father'],
('of', 'B.'): ['C'],
('the', 'father'): ['of', 'of']}

And here is how easy is the Python code for this random text generator:

```
!/usr/bin/env python3
# encoding: utf-8

import sys
from pprint import pprint
from random import choice

EOS = ['.', '?', '!']


def build_dict(words):
```

```python
    """
    Build a dictionary from the
words.

    (word1, word2) => [w1, w2,
...] # key: tuple; value: list
    """
    d = {}
    for i, word in
enumerate(words):
        try:
            first, second, third =
words[i], words[i+1], words[i+2]
        except IndexError:
            break
        key = (first, second)
        if key not in d:
            d[key] = []
        #
        d[key].append(third)
```

```python
    return d


def generate_sentence(d):
    li = [key for key in d.keys()
if key[0][0].isupper()]
    key = choice(li)

    li = []
    first, second = key
    li.append(first)
    li.append(second)
    while True:
        try:
            third = choice(d[key])
        except KeyError:
            break
        li.append(third)
        if third[-1] in EOS:
            break
        # else
```

```python
        key = (second, third)
        first, second = key

    return ' '.join(li)


def main():
    fname = sys.argv[1]
    with     open(fname,        "rt",
encoding="utf-8") as f:
        text = f.read()

    words = text.split()
    d = build_dict(words)
    pprint(d)
    print()
    sent = generate_sentence(d)
    print(sent)
    if sent in text:
        print('# existing sentence
:(')
```

```
######################

if __name__ == "__main__":
    if len(sys.argv) == 1:
        print("Error: provide an
input corpus file.")
        sys.exit(1)
    # else
    main()
```

For best results, choose a longer text. We used 2 words to create our current state. If you choose 3 words, the text generator will be less random sure, but it will also have a lot more meaning than this simple, gibberish example.(6)

Single Speaker Word Recognition

Hidden Markov models have been one of the main components for speech recognition for many years. This chapter will show you a step-by-step way of how to create and implement a code for single speaker speech recognition. And while this may not be the best speech recognizer out there, the example works really well, and it is perfect for providing you a great insight of how hidden Markov models are used for speech recognition, as well as other similar tasks.

Since we obviously need to work on a dataset to prove a point, I used a simple Google Code project. So, let's start, shall we?

```
import numpy as np
import matplotlib.pyplot as plt
```

```python
%matplotlib inline

from utils import progress_bar_downloader
import os

#The zip of the audio can be downloaded here:
link = 'https://dl.dropboxusercontent.com/u/15378192/audio.tar.gz'
dlname = 'audio.tar.gz'

if not os.path.exists('./%s' % dlname):
    progress_bar_downloader(link, dlname)
    os.system('tar xzf %s' % dlname)
else:
```

```
    print('%s already downloaded!'
% dlname)
audio.tar.gz already downloaded!
In [3]:
fpaths = []
labels = []
spoken = []
for f in os.listdir('audio'):
    for w in os.listdir('audio/' +
f):
        fpaths.append('audio/' + f
+ '/' + w)
        labels.append(f)
        if f not in spoken:
            spoken.append(f)
print('Words spoken:', spoken)
```

The data has 7 words: apple, banana, kiwi, lime, orange, peach, and pineapple. Each of these words are spoken 15 times, which results in 105 files. Next, we extract the files into a single data matrix and create a label vector that has the right label for each of the data files.

```
from scipy.io import wavfile

data    =    np.zeros((len(fpaths),
32000))
maxsize = -1
for n,file in enumerate(fpaths):
    _, d = wavfile.read(file)
    data[n, :d.shape[0]] = d
    if d.shape[0] > maxsize:
        maxsize = d.shape[0]
data = data[:, :maxsize]

#Each sample file is one row in
data, and has one entry in labels
print('Number  of  files  total:',
data.shape[0])
```

```python
all_labels                                =
np.zeros(data.shape[0])
for         n,         1         in
enumerate(set(labels)):
    all_labels[np.array([i  for  i,
_   in  enumerate(labels)  if  _  ==
1])] = n

print('Labels  and  label  indices',
all_labels)
```

After downloading the data and turning it into an input matrix, the next thing to do is to extract the features of the raw data.

Most systems for speaker recognition use far more advanced processing in order to extract the features that can describe the sound over time, as well as frequency. We, on the other hand, will stick to the simplest example possible in order to understand how it all works.

```
import scipy

def       stft(x,         fftsize=64,
overlap_pct=.5):
    #Modified                   from
http://stackoverflow.com/questions
/2459295/stft-and-istft-in-python
    hop  =  int(fftsize  *  (1  -
overlap_pct))
    w  =  scipy.hanning(fftsize  +
1)[:-1]
    raw  =  np.array([np.fft.rfft(w
*  x[i:i  +  fftsize])  for  i  in
range(0, len(x) - fftsize, hop)])
    return raw[:, :(fftsize // 2)]
```

In order for us to find frequency peaks, we can
use a technique called STFT (Short Time
Fourier Transform). But even though the next
code uses STFT, know that you can easily

substitute this and use the specgram function of matplotlib, instead.

```python
import matplotlib.pyplot as plt
plt.plot(data[0,                    :],
color='steelblue')
plt.title('Timeseries  example  for
%s'%labels[0])
plt.xlim(0, 3500)
plt.xlabel('Time (samples)')
plt.ylabel('Amplitude  (signed  16
bit)')
plt.figure()


# + 1 to avoid log of 0
log_freq           =         20         *
np.log(np.abs(stft(data[0,  :]))  +
1)
print(log_freq.shape)
plt.imshow(log_freq,  cmap='gray',
interpolation=None)
```

```
plt.xlabel('Freq (bin)')
plt.ylabel('Time        (overlapped
frames)')
plt.ylim(log_freq.shape[1])
plt.title('PSD        of        %s
example'%labels[0])
```

Now, we will search for peaks with the help of a moving window:

1. Make a data window with an X length. This example uses 9.
2. Split that window into three: left, center, and right.
3. Apply function (such as mean, max, median, etc.) to every section of that window.
4. If the value of function of the center function is greater than that on the right or left, proceed to the next step. If not go to step 6.

5. If the maximum value is in the center, then you have fount your peak. Make sure to mark it and then continue.

6. Shift the data by a single sample. Repeat.

7. Once you process the entire data there should be peaks detected.

Here is the code implementation of this algorithm:

```
from numpy.lib.stride_tricks
import as_strided

#Peak detection using the
technique described here:
http://kkjkok.blogspot.com/2013/12
/dsp-snippets_9.html
def peakfind(x, n_peaks, l_size=3,
r_size=3, c_size=3, f=np.mean):
```

```python
    win_size = l_size + r_size +
c_size
    shape    =    x.shape[:-1]    +
(x.shape[-1]    -    win_size    +    1,
win_size)
    strides    =    x.strides    +
(x.strides[-1],)
    xs            =            as_strided(x,
shape=shape, strides=strides)
    def is_peak(x):
        centered   =   (np.argmax(x)
== l_size + int(c_size/2))
        l = x[:l_size]
        c   =   x[l_size:l_size   +
c_size]
        r = x[-r_size:]
        passes   =   np.max(c)   >
np.max([f(l), f(r)])
        if centered and passes:
            return np.max(c)
        else:
```

```
        return -1
    r                            =
np.apply_along_axis(is_peak,      1,
xs)
    top = np.argsort(r, None)[::-
1]
    heights = r[top[:n_peaks]]
    #Add l_size and half - 1 of
center size to get to actual peak
location
    top[top > -1] = top[top > -1]
+ l_size + int(c_size / 2.)
    return heights, top[:n_peaks]
In [8]:
plot_data = np.abs(stft(data[20,
:]))[15, :]
values, locs = peakfind(plot_data,
n_peaks=6)
fp = locs[values > -1]
fv = values[values > -1]
```

```
plt.plot(plot_data,
color='steelblue')
plt.plot(fp,          fv,          'x',
color='darkred')
plt.title('Peak location example')
plt.xlabel('Frequency (bins)')
plt.ylabel('Amplitude')
```

Now, you should implement a GMM-HMM and train your HMM with the Baum-Welch algorithm. To avoid repeating such a lengthy code, you can optimize the implementation of the algorithm from before, found in Learning.

Once we detect the peaks for all frames, we will have a three-dimensional numpy array. We divide each of the frames by the sum of the peaks, which forms a 'state probability' in the dataset for each of those frames. In this case, we are creating six states.

```python
from        sklearn.cross_validation
import StratifiedShuffleSplit
sss                                   =
StratifiedShuffleSplit(all_labels,
test_size=0.1, random_state=0)


for n,i in enumerate(all_obs):
    all_obs[n]                        /=
all_obs[n].sum(axis=0)


for   train_index,   test_index   in
sss:
    X_train,        X_test        =
all_obs[train_index,              ...],
all_obs[test_index, ...]
    y_train,        y_test        =
all_labels[train_index],
all_labels[test_index]
print('Size of  training  matrix:',
X_train.shape)
```

```
print('Size of testing matrix:',
X_test.shape)
```

The thing we need to do next is to finally predict those words. In order to do so, we will have to train 7 different GMM HMM models, and then with the help of the maximum likelihood, we will guess each of the spoken words.

```
ys = set(all_labels)
ms = [gmmhmm(6) for y in ys]
_ = [m.fit(X_train[y_train == y,
:, :]) for m, y in zip(ms, ys)]
ps = [m.transform(X_test) for m in
ms]
res = np.vstack(ps)
predicted_labels = np.argmax(res,
axis=0)
missed = (predicted_labels !=
y_test)
```

```
print('Test     accuracy:     %.2f
percent'   %   (100   *   (1  -
np.mean(missed))))
```

The accuracy of our test is over 71 percent, which you have to admit, is pretty decent for a code of this nature. If you want to see if there was some unusual pattern for misclassification if the words, we can take a look at this confusion matrix:

```
from    sklearn.metrics    import
confusion_matrix
cm   =   confusion_matrix(y_test,
predicted_labels)
plt.matshow(cm, cmap='gray')
ax = plt.gca()
_  =  ax.set_xticklabels(["  "]  +
[1[:2] for 1 in spoken])
_  =  ax.set_yticklabels(["  "]  +
spoken)
```

```
plt.title('Confusion        matrix,
single speaker')
plt.ylabel('True label')
plt.xlabel('Predicted label')
```

(7)

Conclusion

Now that you know everything in order to build and train your HMMs, the next step is to open Python and start coding.

I really hope that this book was able to help you see beyond the complexity of Markov models and gain a good insight in order to solve the scientific mysteries that has been bothering you.

Did you find this book helpful? Leave a review and share your thoughts with the other Markov fans.

References

1. **Kirk, Matthew.** *Thoughtful Machine Learning in Python.* s.l. : O'Reilly Media, Inc., 2017.

2. **Wikipedia.** [Online] https://en.wikipedia.org/wiki/Viterbi_algorithm.

3. **Pautomac.** Probabilistic Automata Learning Competition. [Online] http://ai.cs.umbc.edu/icgi2012/challenge/Pautomac/code/pautomac_baumwelch.py.

4. **HmmLearn.** [Online] http://hmmlearn.readthedocs.io/en/latest/index.html.

5. **Kirk, Matthew.** *Thoughtful Machine Learning in Python.* s.l. : O'Reilly Media, Inc., 2017.

6. **Laci, Jabba.** Generating pseudo random text using Markov chains. [Online] 2014. https://pythonadventures.wordpress.com/2014/01/23/generating-pseudo-random-text-using-markov-chains/.

7. **Kastner, Kyle.** Single Speaker Word Recognition With Hidden Markov Models. [Online] 2014. https://kastnerkyle.github.io/posts/single-speaker-word-recognition-with-hidden-markov-models/.